S.T.E.A.M.

THROUGH THE SEASONS

SUMMER

ANNA CLAYBOURNE

First published in Great Britain in 2019 by Wayland
Copyright © Hodder and Stoughton 2019

Senior Commissioning Editor: Melanie Palmer
Design: squareandcircus.co.uk
Illustrations: Supriya Sahai

HB ISBN 978 1 5263 0948 8
PB ISBN 978 1 5263 0949 5

Picture credits: Evgenii And/Shutterstock: 23bl. Mykhailo
Baidala/Shutterstock: 24bl. Chaoss/Shutterstock: 18bg.
Sussi Hj/Shutterstock: 5cl. Alasdair James/Istockphoto: 16bl.
Kingarion/Shutterstock: 27tl. Valeriy Vladimirovich Kirsanov/
Shutterstock: 15tr. mdesigner125/Istockphoto: 10bl. Matee
Nuserm /Shutterstock: 15bc. M. Unal Ozmen/Shutterstock: 29b.
Valentin Sama-Rojo/Shutterstock: 5t. Romm/Shutterstock: 14bl.
shapecharge/Istockphoto: 5cr. Timelynx/Shutterstock: 12bl.
Yanping Wang/Shutterstock: 19c. geert weggen/
Shutterstock: 21tr. Zikatuha/Shutterstock: 7br.
Additional illustrations: Freepik

Every attempt has been made to clear copyright. Should
there be any inadvertent omission please apply to the
publisher for rectification.

Printed in China

Wayland
An imprint of
Hachette Children's Group
Part of Hodder and Stoughton
Carmelite House
50 Victoria Embankment
London EC4Y 0DZ

An Hachette UK Company
www.hachette.co.uk

SAFETY INFORMATION:
Please ask an adult for help with
any activities that could be tricky,
involve cooking or handling
glass. Ask adult permission when
appropriate.

Due care has been taken to ensure
the activities are safe and the
publishers regret they cannot
accept liability for any loss or
injuries sustained.

Summer festivals

The longest day of summer is called the summer solstice. In the northern hemisphere it's the 21 June, and in the southern hemisphere it's the 21 December. People around the world celebrate around this time with parties and festivals, like the Night of Fire in Spain, and Beliye Nochi (White Nights) in St Petersburg, Russia.

Jumping over a bonfire during Spain's Night of Fire festival. Don't try this at home!

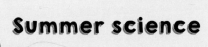

Midsummer celebrations in Sweden

Summer science

This book is full of fun science experiments, activities and things to make in summer.

You can do most of them with everyday craft materials and recycled objects from around the house. Turn to page 30 for some extra tips about materials and where to find them.

HAVE AN ADULT HANDY!

SOME OF THE ACTIVITIES INVOLVE SHARP OBJECTS, HEAT AND COOKING. MAKE SURE YOU ALWAYS HAVE AN ADULT TO HELP YOU, AND ASK THEM TO DO THESE PARTS.

SUN PRINTS

Use the summer sun to make your own simple photo prints, using everyday objects.

WHAT YOU NEED:

- DARK-COLOURED SUGAR PAPER (ALSO CALLED CONSTRUCTION PAPER), SUCH AS PURPLE, DARK BLUE OR DARK RED
- FLAT OBJECTS, SUCH AS COINS, BUTTONS, LEAVES, KEYS OR SHAPES CUT OUT OF CARD
- A BRIGHT SUNNY WINDOWSILL

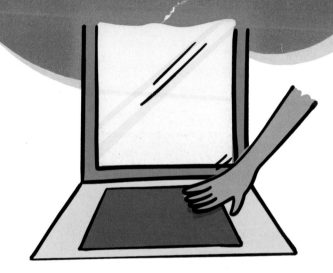

Step 1:
Put a sheet of dark sugar paper on the windowsill, where the sun will shine on it.

Step 2:
Arrange objects on the paper to make a picture or pattern. Make sure they can't roll off or move around.

Step 3:
Leave the paper and objects in the sun for at least a day, if it's very sunny, or for several days if it's less sunny.

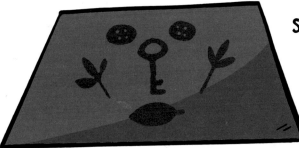

Step 4:

When the paper looks faded, the print is ready. Take the objects away, and you'll see their shapes left behind.

Sunlight contains high-energy UV (ultraviolet) rays.

Summer science:
Drawing with light

This is a kind of very simple photograph. The word "photograph" means "light drawing", and it works using paper that changes colour when light hits it. Sugar paper does the same thing, but much more slowly.

UV rays can break down some types of dye found in paper. The dye becomes less good at soaking up sunlight, so it fades and looks lighter.

Where objects block the sunlight, the paper stays darker.

What else can I make?
You can buy special Sun Print paper that does this too. Look out for it in hobby stores.

MAKE A GNOMON

You can put a gnomon in your garden, but it's nothing to do with gnomes! A gnomon is a kind of shadow clock, invented thousands of years ago.

WHAT YOU NEED:

- A LONG, STRAIGHT STICK
- A PLANT POT OR SMALL BUCKET
- SAND OR STONES
- A SUNNY GARDEN OR OTHER OUTDOOR SPACE
- A WATCH OR SMARTPHONE
- LARGE PEBBLES
- MARKER PENS OR CHALK STICKS

Step 1:

Stand the stick in the plant pot or bucket, surrounded by sand or stones.

Step 2:

Put the gnomon in a place that's in the sun for most of the day, with plenty of space around it.

Step 3:

Now use the watch or smartphone to mark the time. On the hour (at 10 o'clock, 11 o'clock, and so on), put a pebble on the ground where the stick's shadow is.

Summer science: Moving shadows

During the day, the sun seems to move across the sky. It doesn't really. In fact, the sun stays still, and the Earth spins, making the sun appear in different positions. This means that shadows change position too, and we can use them to show the time.

Step 4:

Mark the time on the pebble, using chalk or a marker pen. If the sun isn't out all day, it may take a few days to mark all the hours.

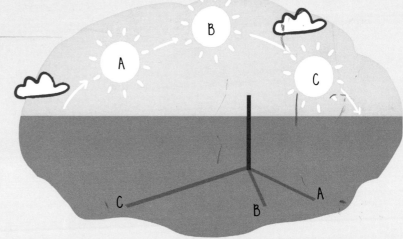

Step 5:

When the gnomon is finished, you can use it to tell the time

What else can I make?

Can you make a mini-gnomon, using a paper plate and a pencil, that can be used indoors?

MINI LIGHTNING

Summer isn't always sunny and bright – it's also famous for its thunderstorms and lightning. Make your own tiny flash of lightning with a spoon and a balloon!

WHAT YOU NEED:

- A BALLOON
- A METAL SPOON
- A ROOM THAT YOU CAN MAKE COMPLETELY DARK
- A SOFT, DRY WOOLLY JUMPER OR SCARF
- A RUBBER GLOVE

Step 1:

Go into the room where you will make the lightning, and stand near the light switch so you can reach it easily.

Step 2:

Blow up the balloon and tie it closed. Put the rubber glove on one hand, and hold the balloon in the other.

Summer science: What is lightning?

When you rub the balloon, it collects electric charge. When the spoon gets close enough, the charge is released, making a spark jump across the gap.

Real lightning happens in the same way, but the spark is MUCH bigger and hotter. Electric charge builds up inside clouds, and the spark jumps between the clouds and the ground.

Step 3:

Rub the balloon quickly to and fro on the woolly sweater or scarf for about a minute. (Or you can rub it on your hair instead.)

Step 4:

Pick up the spoon in your gloved hand, and turn off the light. Slowly, move the end of the spoon towards the balloon.

As it gets closer, a little lightning spark should jump across the gap.

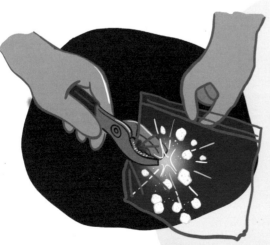

What else can I do?

For another kind of spark, put sugar cubes in a plastic food bag, and ask an adult to crush them with a pair of pliers in a dark room. When sugar gets crushed, it releases light called triboluminescence.

BEE HOTEL

Honeybees make their own nests, but some bees, called solitary bees, make their nests in tubes or tunnels. This bee hotel will help them out.

WHAT YOU NEED:

- AN OLD, LARGE TEA MUG
- BROWN PAPER OR BROWN PAPER BAGS
- SCISSORS
- STRING
- PENCILS AND PENS
- A FENCE OR TREE THAT IS IN THE SUN IN THE MORNING

Step 1:

Wash the mug well and leave it to dry. Cut a piece of string about 30 cm long, thread it through the handle and tie in a knot.

Step 2:

Cut the brown paper or bags into wide strips, and roll them up around pencils and pens to make tubes of different thicknesses.

Summer science:
Bee babies

When a solitary bee finds a good tube to nest in, she lays her eggs inside, along with pollen for the babies (larvae) to eat, and seals the tube up with mud. The babies hatch and grow, then emerge from the tube as adult bees.

Step 3:

Fold each tube over at one end, and cut the other end off to make the tube short enough to fit inside the mug.

Step 5:

Hang the bee hotel up on a fence or tree (ask an adult to help). It should rest against the surface so it doesn't sway in the wind, and point slightly downwards.

Step 4:

Fill the mug with paper tubes, with the folded ends at the bottom. The tubes should be a bit shorter than the mug, to help them stay dry.

What else can I do?

After being used, the bee hotel will be dirty and won't attract new bees. Each year, at the start of summer, throw away the paper tubes, clean out the container and make a new hotel.

MOTH MEET-UP

On warm summer nights, moths fly around in search of food or a mate. Take a closer look at moths using this method, which is called "mothing".

WHAT YOU NEED:

- A GARDEN OR OTHER SAFE OUTDOOR AREA
- A PLAIN WHITE BED SHEET
- A WASHING LINE OR LONG, LOW TREE BRANCH
- CLOTHES PEGS
- A BRIGHT TORCH
- A PICNIC MAT
- A DARK, DRY, CALM NIGHT
- NOTEBOOK AND PENS

Step 1:

You have to do this in the dark, so wait until night falls, and make sure you're dressed warmly.

Step 2:

With an adult to help, hang the sheet up over the washing line or tree branch, using clothes pegs to hold it in place.

Step 3:

Spread out the picnic rug near the sheet, and shine the torch at the middle of the sheet. Gradually, moths should come and settle on the sheet.

Step 4:

If you have a spotter's guide book, use it to try to identify the moths. Or you could try taking photographs of them, or sketching them with a pencil and notebook.

Summer science:
Flying by night

While butterflies come out in the daytime, most moths are active at night. They are attracted to bright lights, though scientists are not sure why. The brightly lit sheet attracts the moths and gives them a place to rest as well.

What else can I do?

Try mothing in other places too, such as when you're camping, or at a relative's house. Do you see different types of moth?

BEACH ART

Several great artists have made art on beaches using natural objects. Have a go at this yourself on a day at the beach. Here are some projects to try...

WHAT YOU NEED:
- A BEACH
- ROCKS, PEBBLES, SEA GLASS, SEASHELLS AND OTHER BEACH OBJECTS

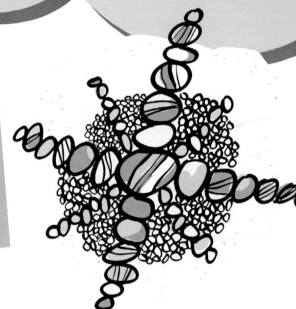

1. Abstract patterns
Arrange pebbles and shells to make stars, hearts, spirals, grids or other shapes. Try sorting them into shades and colours to make shadow or rainbow effects.

Summer science:
Smoothed by the sea

Why are beach pebbles so smooth and rounded? As waves crash on the beach, they roll and tumble rocks around. They grind together and get smoothed down. The same thing happens to pieces of glass, turning them into smooth, soft-cornered sea glass.

2. Beach pictures

Make a portrait of someone you know, or a picture of a sea creature. Seaweed makes good hair!

Here today, gone tomorrow

When the tide comes in, it will wash away your beach art. Remember to take photos of your masterpieces before you go home!

3. Rock towers

Use flat rocks or pebbles to make amazing towers and pyramids. How many can you balance in a tower? Hold a contest with your friends or family.

Try this type of tower too:

When you've finished, remember to put the pebbles back where you found them!

What else can I make?

Can you make an archway of pebbles that holds itself up, like this?

SAND SECRETS

Have you ever wondered what sand is, and where it comes from? Take a closer look, and try doing a sandy science experiment.

Step 1:

First, put some sand on a flat surface, so you can look at it closely through the magnifying glass.

WHAT YOU NEED:

- SAND (FROM A SANDY BEACH, A RIVER BEACH OR EVEN A SANDPIT)
- A STRONG MAGNIFYING GLASS
- A SMALL PLATE
- VINEGAR OR LEMON JUICE
- A TEASPOON

Rock
Seashell
Coral
Glass

Step 2:

What can you see? Look for different colours, shapes and sizes of grains of sand. Are there any objects you recognise? Can you identify any of these things?

Step 3:

Now put some sand on the plate in a little pile. Fill the teaspoon with vinegar or lemon juice, and gently pour it onto the sand.

Step 4:

Watch carefully. Does the sand fizz or bubble, or does it stay unchanged?

Sand grains under a microscope

Summer science:
Types of sand

Sand can be made of several different ingredients, sometimes all mixed together. Some is mostly made from rock, such as quartz. Some is made from seashells or coral. Over time, water, wind and weather wear these things down, breaking them into tiny sand grains.

Seashells and coral contain a mineral called calcium. It reacts with acids, like vinegar or lemon juice, to make gas bubbles. If sand fizzes in acid, you know it contains a lot of these animal materials.

What else can I make?

If you have a microscope, try using that to take an even closer look at sand. Can you see any tiny bits of plastic? In some places, sand is polluted with plastic from human-made objects.

NATURE PAINTS

In summer, it's easy to find all kinds of colourful fruit and vegetables, like berries, cherries, mangoes and salad leaves. As well as eating them, you can use them to make natural paints.

WHAT YOU NEED:
- BRIGHTLY COLOURED FRUITS AND VEGETABLES (SEE CHART BELOW)
- A KITCHEN KNIFE AND CHOPPING BOARD
- A HAND BLENDER, A PESTLE AND MORTAR, OR A POTATO MASHER
- BOWLS
- A SIEVE
- A SPOON
- PAPER
- PAINTBRUSHES

Step 1:
Choose some fruits and vegetables to try making into paints. The chart below shows which ones work best.

Step 2:
If you've chosen something large like a mango, ask an adult to chop it into smaller pieces. Then ask them to blend the fruit or veg for a few seconds with the blender. If you don't have a blender, grind it up with a pestle and mortar, or mash it in a bowl with a potato masher.

Green:
SPINACH
MINT
KALE
PARSLEY

Purples, pinks and reds:
BLUEBERRIES
BLACKCURRANTS
BLACKBERRIES
CHERRIES
RASPBERRIES
STRAWBERRIES
COOKED BEETROOT

Oranges and yellows:
TOMATOES
MANGOES

Step 3:

Put the sieve over a clean bowl. Put your mushed-up fruit or veg in the sieve, and stir it with a spoon to push the juice through into the bowl.

Summer science:
Eat me please!

Why are so many fruits and berries brightly coloured? Plants grow bright fruits and berries that stand out from the surrounding leaves, to help animals to find them more easily. When birds and other animals eat fruits and berries, they help the plants, by spreading the seeds around in their droppings, so they find new places to grow.

Step 4:

Use the same method with different types of fruit and vegetables to create different coloured paints. Now you can try painting with them!

What else can I make?
Kitchen spices can make good paints too. Try turmeric mixed with water for a warm, bright yellow.

EXPLODING CHALK BAG

this is a SERIOUSLY messy experiment to do outdoors in summer. Make sure you get permission to make a mess first!

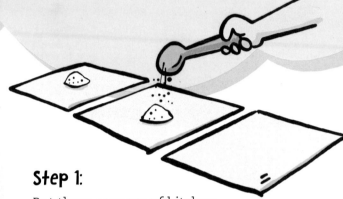

WHAT YOU NEED:

- 3 ZIP-SEALING SANDWICH BAGS
- CORNFLOUR (CORNSTARCH)
- WHITE VINEGAR
- MEASURING JUG
- FOOD COLOURING
- BICARBONATE OF SODA (ALSO CALLED BAKING SODA)
- A TEASPOON
- KITCHEN PAPER
- A HARD OUTDOOR SURFACE, SUCH AS A PATIO OR PLAYGROUND

Step 1:
Put three squares of kitchen paper on a flat surface. Put three teaspoonfuls of baking soda on the middle of each square.

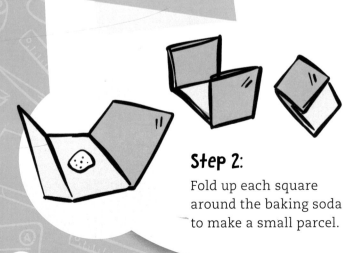

Step 2:
Fold up each square around the baking soda to make a small parcel.

Step 3:
Measure 100 ml of cornflour, and 100 ml of white vinegar, into each sandwich bag. Add a few drops of food colouring to each bag. Seal up the bags so that they can't leak.

Summer science: Gas bags

When the bicarbonate of soda mixes with the vinegar, a chemical reaction happens. The two substances combine and make new chemicals, including a gas, carbon dioxide. As the reaction creates more and more gas, it fills up the bag and makes it pop.

Step 4:

Take everything outdoors, and put the three bags on the ground. Now open one corner of each bag, drop in a parcel of baking soda, and quickly seal the bag up again, ensuring it is airtight.

Step 5:

Make sure the bicarbonate of soda parcel falls into the mixture in the bag. Stand well back!

What else can I make?

Try mixing bicarbonate of soda with vinegar in a bottle. As fast as you can, stretch a balloon over the top. What happens?

CRYSTAL ART

On a hot summer day, things that are wet soon get dry. Wet washing dries in the sun. Puddles dry up on the hot ground. You can also use the warm, drying sunshine to make crystal art!

WHAT YOU NEED:

- KITCHEN SALT
- A LARGE SPOON
- A MIXING JUG
- WARM WATER
- FOOD COLOURING
- PEBBLES
- LARGE SHEETS OF PAPER
- A SAFE AREA OUTDOORS
- A HOT, SUNNY DAY

Step 1:

Put several spoonfuls of salt in the jug. Add enough hot tap water to cover the salt. Mix it well until the salt has disappeared.

Summer science:
Evaporation

As water warms up, it evaporates. That means it changes from a liquid into a gas, called water vapour, and floats away into the air. If salt is dissolved in the water, it gets left behind, and forms shapes called crystals. Try looking at them through a magnifying glass.

Step 2:

Add a few drops of food colouring to colour your salt mixture, and stir it in well.

Step 3:

Outside, spread a large sheet of paper on the ground. Use pebbles to hold the corners down.

Step 4:

Gently pour salt mixture onto the middle of the paper to make a puddle. (Don't worry if some runs off.) Leave it in the sun to dry.

Step 5:

As the water dries, it leaves colourful salt crystal patterns behind.

What else can I make?

Try the same experiment with sugar, or Epsom salts, from a chemist's. Do they make different crystals?

Make mixtures in different colours and use them to make a pattern on the paper.

GREENHOUSE EFFECT

Have you ever wondered why it gets so boiling hot inside a greenhouse, or inside a car with the windows closed, on a sunny day?

WHAT YOU NEED:

- TWO SMALL BARS OF MILK CHOCOLATE
- TWO SMALL PLASTIC BOWLS
- A CLEAR GLASS MIXING BOWL
- A WATCH OR TIMER
- A SUNNY OUTDOOR SPACE, AND A SUNNY DAY

Step 1:

Open the chocolate, break up each bar, and put one bar in one plastic bowl, and one in the other.

Step 2:

Put both the bowls on the ground, where the sun can shine on them.

Step 3:

Turn the glass mixing bowl upside down and carefully put it over one of the bowls.

Summer science: trapped heat

If the sun is shining, you should find that the chocolate starts to melt – but the chocolate under the mixing bowl will melt faster. Sunlight can easily shine through glass. But when it hits objects, it turns into heat. Under the glass bowl, it's much harder for this heat to escape, and it can't mix with the cooler air around it. So the chocolate under the bowl gets hotter faster.

Step 4:

Every five minutes, look at the chocolate inside the bowls. What's happening?

The name "greenhouse effect" is also used to describe the way some gases in the air, such as carbon dioxide, trap heat in the Earth's atmosphere, making the world warm up.

What else can I do?

If you have two garden thermometers, try the same experiment, but with one thermometer under the glass bowl, and one next to it. Can you see a difference in temperature?

ICE CREAM SHAKER

On a hot summer day, an ice cream helps you cool down. But did you know you can make your own ice cream in just a few minutes?

WHAT YOU NEED:

- A SELF-SEAL SANDWICH BAG
- A CUP OF FULL-FAT MILK
- 1 TABLESPOON OF SUGAR
- A DROP OF VANILLA FLAVOURING
- A BAG OF ICE CUBES (FROM A SUPERMARKET, OR MAKE ABOUT 50 ICE CUBES IN A FREEZER AND PUT THEM IN A LARGE FOOD BAG)
- 6 HEAPED TABLESPOONS OF SALT

Step 1:

Mix the milk, sugar and vanilla together in the sandwich bag. Seal it closed, making sure there is not much air trapped inside.

Step 2:

Put the salt into the bag of ice cubes, and shake it to spread the salt around a bit.

Step 3:

Put the sandwich bag into the bag of ice cubes, in the middle so it's surrounded by ice. Seal the bag.

Yum!

Step 4:
Shake the bag of ice cubes for about 5 minutes. If your arms get tired, ask an adult to help.

Step 5:
Take out the smaller bag, and quickly rinse it under a cold tap to get the salt off. Open it and try your ice cream!

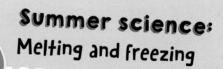

Summer science:
Melting and freezing

The ice on its own would cool the milk down, but it freezes extra-fast because of the salt. The salt lowers the freezing point of water, and this makes the ice cubes start to melt. But melting uses up energy. So the ice cubes take heat energy from the milk, making it cold enough to freeze.

What else can I make?
Try it with flavoured milk, or soya or oat milk.

Or try different flavourings, like mint essence.

MATERIALS

this list gives you ideas about where to look for the materials you need for the activities in this book.

FROM AROUND THE HOUSE:

- COINS
- BUTTONS
- KEYS
- WATCH
- SMARTPHONE
- WOOLLY JUMPER
- BEDSHEET
- CLOTHES PEGS
- WASHING LINE
- TORCHES
- PICNIC RUG
- MAGNIFYING GLASS

BASIC ART AND CRAFT MATERIALS:

- PAPER
- FELT-TIP PENS
- MARKER PENS
- COLOURED PENCILS
- SCISSORS
- GLUE
- STICKY TAPE
- PAINTBRUSHES

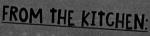

FROM THE KITCHEN:

- GLASSES, BOWLS, JUGS, PLATES AND SAUCERS
- SPOONS
- RUBBER GLOVES
- WATER
- ICE CUBES
- KITCHEN ROLL
- FOOD STORAGE BAGS
- KNIFE AND CHOPPING BOARD
- HAND BLENDER
- PESTLE AND MORTAR
- POTATO MASHER
- SIEVE
- MILK
- SUGAR
- VINEGAR
- LEMON JUICE
- BICARBONATE OF SODA (BAKING SODA)
- FRUIT AND VEGETABLES
- CORNFLOUR (CORNSTARCH)
- FOOD COLOURING
- SALT

FROM A CRAFT OR HOBBY SHOP:

- SUGAR OR CONSTRUCTION PAPER
- CHALK
- BALLOONS

FROM A SUPERMARKET OR GARDEN CENTRE:

- VANILLA FLAVOURING
- CHOCOLATE
- PLANT POTS

FROM A GARDEN OR PARK:

- LEAVES
- STICKS
- PEBBLES

FROM A BEACH:

- SEASHELLS
- SEAWEED
- SAND

Glossary

calcium A mineral found in coral, seashells, bones and teeth.

carbon dioxide A type of gas that is found in the air, and forms in some chemical reactions.

chemical reaction A process that makes some substances change when they mix together.

crystals Minerals that have formed in regular, geometric shapes.

dissolve Solid substances dissolve when they mix into a liquid and break up into invisible bits.

droppings A name for animal poo.

electric charge A store of electrical energy held in a substance or object.

evaporate To change from a liquid into a gas.

freezing point The temperature that a substance freezes at.

gnomon A shadow clock made from an upright stick.

greenhouse effect A global warming effect in which temperatures rise due to gases being trapped in the Earth's atmosphere.

midsummer The middle of summer, when the days are longest and the nights are shortest.

minerals Pure, non-living substances, such as salt, quartz and calcium.

mothing Finding and studying moths.

northern hemisphere The half of the Earth north of the equator, around the North Pole.

orbit To circle around another object, such as a planet orbiting around the sun.

pollen A yellow powder made by flowers, which bees feed on.

quartz A hard mineral found in many types of rock.

react See chemical reaction.

sea glass Pieces of glass that have become smoothed and rounded from being in the sea.

solitary Living and spending time alone. Solitary bees are types of bees that live on their own instead of in beehives or colonies.

southern hemisphere The half of the Earth south of the equator, around the South Pole.

summer solstice The longest day of summer.

thermometer An instrument that measures the temperature.

triboluminescence Light that is released when some types of substances are crushed, squeezed or stretched.

UV (ultraviolet) A type of light ray that cannot be seen by human eyes, but is found in sunlight.

water vapour Water in the form of a gas. Water vapour is found in the air and released by plants.

Index